alex theo

illustrated by emily chandler

Dedication

To every family member, friend, and stranger who has supported and believed in me and my dreams, thank you. This is for you.

Dear Reader,

Thank you.

Thank you for picking up my book. You have no idea how truly grateful I am for you. No matter if someone you love gave this to you, or you simply felt called to pick it up off the shelf, this book was meant to find you. These words were written from my heart and soul, to help bring light and love to yours.

My story was easy to write, because Odie and the old man are me—and also you. They represent all of us and our shared experience of being beautiful souls that walk this earth in human bodies. It is my sincere hope that you resonate with Odie and the old man as much as I did when creating them. May the old man's wisdom help illuminate whatever path you may be on, and may Odie's pure love restore even a bit of your faith in this world.

The recipe included at the end of the book is one I have been perfecting for years. I always swore I would keep it a secret, but I thought sharing it with you, my dear reader, would be the only appropriate thank you for picking up my book. I've always found food to be the greatest tool for connection, and so my only request is this: should you choose to follow my recipe and make a pot of avgolemono, make it for those you love—whether it be family, friends, or even a self-love evening by yourself.

Now, that's enough from me—I'll let Odie and the old man take it from here. May their journey together leave you hopeful, inspired, and just a little hungry.

All my love,

Alex Theo xx

Food is our common ground,
a universal experience.

— James Beard —

On an island
in the Mediterranean.

"I want to make soup," said Odie to no one.

"Then make soup!" replied a calming voice.

Odie spun around to find an old man standing in the doorway of the kitchen. The man was tall, with thick, grey hair tied back into a bun. He had twinkling green eyes gazing at Odie from behind a pair of bright orange spectacles, and a kind smile resting peacefully on his face.

"Who are you?" asked Odie.

"The question is, who are you?"

Odie clasped his hands together and looked down at the floor, shyly swaying side to side.

"My name is Odie," he said.

The old man kept smiling.

"Hi, Odie. You said you'd like to make soup?"

Odie nodded.

"Yes, that's right. But I can't reach the cupboard with all of my mamá's recipes. It's too tall!" He spun back around and pointed at the tall cupboard to the right of the sink. "See?"

The old man's gaze followed Odie's pointer finger.

"Ah, I see. That is quite tall, isn't it?" The old man looked around the kitchen and grabbed a step stool sitting in the corner. He picked it up and brought it to the counter, helping Odie climb up onto the stool.

"Never be afraid to ask others for help."

Odie nodded, reaching to open the cupboard. He let out a big sigh.

"What's wrong?" asked the old man.

"There are just so many soup recipes!" said Odie, throwing his hands into the air in exasperation. "I don't know how I'll ever choose the right one to make."

The old man laughed softly, smiling up at Odie.

"Life is full of many choices. I promise that if you always listen to your heart, you will never be led astray."

"How do you listen to your heart?" Odie asked.

The old man smiled.

"Close your eyes and let out the biggest breath you can."

Odie nodded and closed his eyes, letting out a big exhale.

"Now take a deep breath in, and gently blow out." The old man paused. "What's your heart saying?"

Odie smiled as he listened to his heart.

"How about avgolemono?"

The old man smiled. "That's my favorite soup."

Odie flung open his eyes and spun around on the stool, laughing. "Mine too!" He paused for a moment, looking down at the man. "I think I know you."

The old man just smiled. "You do."

Odie grabbed the recipe and hopped down, dragging the stool to the kitchen table. The old man took a seat next to him.

Odie started reading the recipe. "Oh my," he sighed, "there are so many things to do."

The old man nodded. "There are indeed. Do you know what I like to do when I'm overwhelmed?"

Odie looked up at the old man. "What?"

"Take things one ingredient at a time."

Odie nodded.

Odie and the old man read through the entire recipe together, from start to finish. They made a list of all the ingredients and equipment they needed.

"Now, let's begin the mise en place."

"Mise en place?" asked Odie.

The old man smiled and said, "Mise en place. It means 'everything in its place.' Similar to in the kitchen, the Universe has its own mise en place for you. You must remember that everything is always in its place, as are you. You are always exactly where you are meant to be."

Odie nodded.

Together, they got to work. As the old man put the whole chicken into the pot, Odie started to cry.

"I feel sad."

The old man knelt beside him.

"Well, that is certainly valid and I'm proud of you for voicing it." The old man gave Odie a hug.

"What may you be sad about?"

Odie sniffled and looked back down into the pot.

"The chicken gave its life so we could make soup."

The old man looked up at Odie with his kind eyes shining bright.

"You have a compassionate and caring soul. That can make this world feel tougher or harder than it actually is. It may sometimes feel like a weakness, but please know it is one of your greatest strengths." He paused, then added, "Don't let anyone take that away."

Odie nodded.

"You know, we can thank the chicken for giving its life," said the old man.

"How?"

"Every being is made of energy, and energy can never be created nor destroyed. If you send gratitude to the energy of this chicken, I promise it will feel it."

Odie nodded and rested his hand on the pot.

"Thank you, Mr. Chicken."

The old man smiled and stood up again. "Gratitude is the most important form of exercise we can practice. Always remember to be grateful above all else."

Odie nodded.

They filled the pot with chicken stock and water to cover the bird. Odie threw the carrots, celery, onions, garlic, cinnamon, bay leaves, oregano, salt, and peppercorns into the pot.

"Ergh, this is heavy!" Odie exclaimed as he tried to move the pot to the stove.

"Heavy things are always easier to lift when you let others help you. Here," said the old man, as he helped him carry the pot to the stove.

"Thanks," said Odie.

The old man turned the flame on the stove to high and Odie jumped back.

"Agh!" shouted Odie, covering his eyes.

"It's okay to be scared. Sometimes things can be big and scary," said the old man. He turned down the flame. "But you are brave, and strong, and you can do big and scary things."

Odie nodded, then looked down at the recipe.

"We have to let that simmer for an hour. That's forever!"

The old man smiled. "Good things in life are worth waiting for."

The old man and the boy sat down at the table as the broth began to simmer. Odie started absentmindedly tapping his fingers on the table. The old man grabbed an empty pot and flipped it upside down, playing the pot like a hand drum, synchronizing to Odie's beat. He started whistling a melody to go along, and what a song it was. The boy looked up in glee at the old man, giggling.

"There is great joy to be had in creating something out of nothing, like music, with friends," said the old man with a smile.

Odie nodded in agreement.

The old man looked out the window, the Mediterranean Sea sparkling in the sunlight reflecting off the water's turquoise blue surface.

"Let's go outside while we wait."

Odie and the old man stepped into the daylight, looking out at the sea that expanded beyond the horizon.

"Sometimes I feel small when I look out into the world," said Odie, his green eyes twinkling in the light.

"I don't think you'll ever lose that wonder," smiled the old man. "You may be small in the vastness of our Universe, but you are also immensely powerful. Never forget that."

Odie nodded.

He and the old man continued walking, following the path down to the water. There were a couple of kids about Odie's age, playing with a ball by the water.

Odie looked at them before looking up at the old man and noting, "I'm different from them."

"Different is good."

Odie looked down at the ground.

"I don't like to play ball like they do."

"Ah, I see. What is it you like to do?"

Odie thought for a moment before smiling. "Make soup."

The old man smiled. "Me too. That's the beautiful thing about humans, isn't it?"

"What is?" asked Odie, looking up at the man.

"We all have different things that light our souls on fire." He pointed at the girls playing with the ball. "For them, it may be playing ball. And maybe for him, it's bringing music into this world," he said as he pointed to a boy practicing the flute on a bench.

He looked down at Odie and smiled.

"For you and me, perhaps it's making soup. Whatever it is, no matter how different from anyone else, always chase after what sets your soul on fire. Do that and you will certainly find joy."

Odie nodded.

Odie and the old man kept walking along the sea.

"What if I made the chicken broth wrong?" asked Odie. "And what if the avgolemono comes out awful?"

"It's perfectly natural to look back on the past with what-ifs, or be concerned with the uncertainties of the future," replied the old man. The old man dropped a knee to the earth below him and scooped three small holes in the sand with his hands. He pointed to the hole all the way on the left.

"This one represents our past."

He pointed to the one all the way to the right.

"And this one, our future. This," he pointed to the middle hole, "represents the present moment.

He pulled a bucket seemingly out of thin air, and dipped it into the Mediterranean Sea, filling it with water as clear as glass. "This water represents all the energy we have to give. Where we choose to let our thoughts linger is where we pour our precious water. If we choose to dwell upon moments in our past, constantly asking ourselves 'What if I did this' or 'Chose this instead,' the past is where we are putting our energy." He poured some of the sea water into the first hole, the water splashing against the sides of the sand.

"Same with when we lose ourselves amid the uncertainties of what lies ahead," he continued, as he let a stream of water fill the third hole.

"But it is never wise to dwell upon what has come or is to come, for what has come is gone, and what is to come will be. It is a waste of our water to fill these two holes.

"However, when we allow ourselves to remain truly present, we are choosing to fill this hole." He pointed to the middle. As he emptied the rest of the bucket of water into the second hole in the sand, the water glistened like never before, a golden light radiating out of the sand. The boy watched the water in amazement, the old man smiling softly next to him.

"Though we will always have the choice of where to pour our water, we only ever have right now. Our mission must be to remain grounded, stay present, and pour as much of our water into the present moment as possible."

The boy thought to himself for a moment, the reflection of the golden light in the hole in the sand shimmering across his face.

"I think I get it. But how do I do that? How do I pour my water into the present?"

The old man looked down and smiled.

"You meditate."

Odie looked up, confused. "I what?"

The old man laughed. "You bring your heart into the present. Come, I'll show you."

Odie and the old man sat down on the rocks by the sea, a few feet apart from one another, each sitting cross-legged with their hands in their laps.

"Now put your right hand on your heart, and your left hand on your belly," instructed the old man. "Remember what we did earlier when you listened to your heart?"

Odie thought for a moment. "I closed my eyes, blew out all the air I had, and then took a big breath in."

The old man smiled. "Precisely! We do the same thing to bring our hearts into the present."

Odie and the old man closed their eyes, exhaled, and then took a deep inhale.

"Now let it all out."

As they blew the air out of their lips, the wind coming off the sea blew with them.

"Do you feel that breeze?" asked the old man.

"Yes."

"As it blows, let it take any stress you are holding of the past and any worry you have of the future away with the exhalation of your breath. Visualize it going from your heart, out your mouth with your breath, and let it be swept away with the wind."

Odie nodded as he breathed out all of his worries.

The breeze picked up, swirling around Odie and the old man. If there was any passerby, they may have noticed the boy and the old man seemed to be levitating a few inches off the ground. They also may have seen the kaleidoscope of cerulean blue butterflies fluttering amongst the winds, the sunset radiating on them like a spotlight from the universe. A sight, if witnessed, that would immediately disprove anyone who didn't believe in the existence of magic. Alas, no such passerby was there to witness such a sight (though what a magical sight it was).

"I feel it," said Odie.

"Feel what?"

"I feel my heart coming into the present."

The old man smiled.

"Shall we go finish our soup?"

Odie nodded.

As they stood up and started walking back to the house, Odie looked up at the old man.

"You know a lot about a lot of things," he remarked.

"So do you, even if you may not realize it yet. You harbor great wisdom within you—ask yourself for guidance and I promise you can tap into that wisdom whenever you need," said the old man.

Odie nodded, smiling softly at himself.

They walked in silence the rest of the way back to the house, both boy and man lost in their respective thoughts. Once inside, they got back to work.

As the old man took the broth off the stove, he burnt himself on the hot pot.

"Ouch," he whispered to himself.

"You got hurt!" exclaimed Odie.

The old man nodded. "I did indeed. But every wound will eventually heal. It just needs time," he turned on the faucet to run the burn under cold water, "and a little bit of love and care."

The boy nodded.

The rest of the recipe was a beautiful ballet between the boy and old man, each next step taken with effortless ease and grace. Odie dumped the rice in the pot and began juicing the lemons whilst the old man separated the eggs and began to whip the whites.

"Lemons are sour," remarked Odie, as he squeezed the juice out.

The old man nodded in agreement. "True." He reached over and grabbed a slice of lemon, and took a bite. His mouth puckered at the acidic intrusion, his eyes

squinting shut, the wrinkles in the cor-
ners of his eyes jumping out. "OoOH!" He
shouted and laughed, his body dancing in
a shimmy.

Odie stared in amusement, giggling
with glee at the sight.

"What'd you do that for?!" laughed
Odie.

"Sometimes in life, things will be sour.
That's an inevitable part of the human
experience," explained the old man. "But
what we *can* control is how we react to
the sourness. Learn to embrace it, look
for the joys despite it, and you will find it
packs far less of a punch."

Odie grabbed a lemon slice and popped it in his mouth.

"And do it with friends—that makes the sour sweet."

The old man smiled to himself. "Agreed."

After some time had gone by, Odie looked at the old man whipping the egg whites with concern.

"If your wrist is tired, we can switch. Sometimes even small things can be hard. That's what friends are for," said Odie.

The old man looked at Odie with a mix of admiration, amusement, and appreciation.

"You are absolutely right, Odie. You know, you just reminded me of a very important lesson."

"What's that?" Odie asked as he grabbed the whisk from the old man and continued to whip the whites.

"There is no age too great to stop learning, nor is there an age too young to be a teacher. Thank you for sharing your wisdom with me, Odie."

Odie just smiled and pulled up his whisk, the egg white dripping off forming a perfectly soft peak.

"Done!"

They mixed in the egg yolks, then the lemon juice. They temped it up with some of the hot broth, and then Odie slowly poured it into the pot while the old man vigorously stirred, integrating the fluffy lemon and egg mixture with the creamy chicken and rice soup. The egg yolks turned the whole pot a gorgeous sunshine yellow, the silky smooth consistency of the soup gently kissing the sides of the pot as they stirred. An aroma no words could describe wafted out, filling the kitchen and dancing its way into every corner of the home. Warm notes of cinnamon tangoed with the vibrant aroma of the lemon juice, each ingredient playing a crucial part in the delicate balance of the soup. Odie and the old man looked at one another, both with a smile ear-to-ear, positively intoxicated by their co-creation that stood before them.

The old man ladled piping-hot portions into their bowls and they sat down at the kitchen table, side by side, friend by friend. The sun was nearly set, the dark blue sky beyond the water painted brilliant shades of orange, pink, and purple.

"Thanks," said Odie.

"For what?" asked the old man.

"For teaching me how to listen to my heart. And how to give thanks to the chicken. And bring my heart into the present." He paused and smiled. "And for making soup with me. I had the most lovely day with you."

The old man beamed at Odie. "I, too, am incredibly grateful for our day together. Thank you for listening to your heart, and giving thanks to the chicken, and bringing your heart into the present. And for making soup with me. It's been a joy.

"Now, shall we?" He lifted his spoon-
ful of soup and made a cheers gesture to
Odie.

They took their first bite, and immediately felt the warmth spread through
their bodies, from their throats, to their
hearts, down to their toes. It felt like a
golden light pouring through each of
them, liquid gold cascading like a water-
fall. It filled up every corner of their souls
and bodies.

"Do you feel that?" asked the old man.

Odie fervently nodded and looked up
at the man with great curiosity.

"What is it?"

"The most important ingredient in this soup is one we didn't prep for: it's love. Whatever you do in life, Odie, do it with great love, for the outcome will always come out better. If you always cook with love the way we did together today, your food will never be short of sublime. I promise."

"We did cook with love today," replied Odie. He paused for a moment, then continued. "I love you, but I don't know you."

The old man smiled. "To feel is to know. And you do know me—I'm you."

Odie looked up into the old man's green eyes and felt his love, and so he understood what a part of him knew all along. The old man was indeed Odie, just many years in the future.

"How are you here with me now?" asked the boy.

"I am always with you, just as you are always with me. You see, time is not linear. We can access every version of ourselves at all times. I can come here and send you love, just as easily as you can come to me and gain wisdom or strength whenever you need." He paused for a moment and smiled to him-self. "And as we've learned today, vice versa."

Odie nodded.

He and the old man finished their bowls of soup, savoring every last bite.

"I have to go now," said the old man, as he placed his spoon in the empty bowl in front of him.

Odie looked up with tears in his eyes.

"I don't want you to go yet!"

"We will always have each other," said the old man with a smile. "I promise."

"But how will I find you again?" asked Odie with a sniffle.

The old man knelt down on one knee to place himself at eye level. He reached out his wrinkled hand and placed it on Odie's chest.

"I live in here," he said with a soft smile. "Anytime you need me, just listen to your heart like we practiced today, and there I will be."

He embraced Odie in a hug.

"Promise me you'll dream beyond your wildest dreams," he whispered in his ear. "And even when it feels scary, and regardless of anyone who says you can't, you'll have the courage to pursue them."

Odie nodded and sniffled, wiping the tears from his eyes.

"I promise."

The front door opened and closed, and a woman's voice carried down the hall.

"Odie, I'm home!"

The old man's eyes welled with tears, and his hand flew instantly to his heart.

"Mamá's voice... I- I haven't heard it in years."

Odie thought for a moment, looking up into the old man's wrinkled face.

"If I'm always with you, and you're always with me," asked Odie, "and if we were able to send thanks to the chicken because his energy always exists," he continued, "doesn't that mean Mamá is always with you too? And since her energy is always around us, you can always send her love?"

The old man gave Odie another hug, a little tighter this time, a tear falling down his cheek.

"You're absolutely right. Thank you, Odie. Now, go, give your mamá a hug!"

Odie ran down the hallway laughing, jumping into his mother's arms. When they turned the corner back into the kitchen, the old man was gone. There was just a note on the table, next to his empty bowl.

It's going to be a good life, kid. One filled with laughter, love, and lots and lots of soup. xx

HOME

Avgolemono Recipe

Ingredients	Amount
Chicken, whole	1 each
Chicken stock	4 cups
Water	12 cups
Carrots, quartered	5 each
Celery stalks, quartered	5 each
Garlic bulb	1 each
Cinnamon stick	1 each
Bay leaves	3 each
Oregano, dried	2 Tbsp
Black peppercorns	½ tsp
Sea salt, coarse	2 Tbsp
Yellow onions, quartered	2 each
Arborio rice, uncooked	1.5 cups
Eggs, separated	4 each
Lemon juice	1.5 cups, fresh (plus more to taste)

METHOD

1 Place chicken in the pot with carrots, celery, garlic, cinnamon, bay leaves, oregano, salt, and onion. Cover with chicken stock and water. Let cook for one hour.

2 Strain the broth. You can either shred the chicken and add it back to the soup later, or you can serve it in whole pieces on the side of the soup with lemon juice and salt. Compost or repurpose the cooked vegetables.

3 Add rice to the pot, let cook on low flame for about 40 min. Turn off flame.

4 Separate egg whites and yolks, whip whites until you get soft peaks. Add yolks one at a time while beating. Slowly add lemon juice.

5 Temper the egg mixture with the soup (add some of the hot broth to the mixture to slowly raise the temperature). Add the whole mixture to the soup and stir vigorously.

6 Add back shredded chicken, if desired. Bring soup to temperature and serve with extra lemon. Share with those you love

ALEX THEO has been a storyteller his whole life. In second grade, he got in trouble for writing short stories in his notebook during recess instead of playing with the other kids on the playground.

Theo received his BSBA in Marketing and Leadership Studies from Elon University in Elon, North Carolina. It was at Elon his spiritual healing journey began, as he began to accept and love his identity as a gay man. Following his heart and believing in divine guidance, he went back to school to receive a second degree in Culinary Arts from the Culinary Institute of America in Napa Valley, California. Theo brings a unique blend of creativity and expertise to his literary pursuits. Through his words, he invites readers to savor the richness of simply being, blending the flavors of culinary artistry with the magic of the Universe. Theo's only hope for his stories is to inspire readers and spread light in this world.

When he's not writing or cooking in his kitchen in Raleigh, North Carolina, you can find Theo booking a flight to a new country, in search of good food and better stories.